VINCENT'S AMAZING ALGORITHM

How Software Goes Bad

MICHELE DOWNS

Copyright © 2014 Michele C. Downs
All rights reserved.

ISBN: 1500882453
ISBN 13: 9781500882457

To Xander, Dawson, Josie, Theo, Eric, and Simone.

CONTENTS

The Disaster · 1
A Dazzling Solution · 4
Unforeseen Problems Show Up · · · · · · · · · · · · · 7
Vincent Tries to Find a New Approach · · · · · · · · · 9
Tabby Helps Out · 11
More about Lemmings · · · · · · · · · · · · · · · · · · · 14
Tabby Solves the Geometry Problem · · · · · · · · · · 17
Tabby Gets Things Moving · · · · · · · · · · · · · · · · · 20
Tabby Solves the Timing Problem · · · · · · · · · · · 25
Quitters! · 27
And So the Story Ends · · · · · · · · · · · · · · · · · · · 29
About the Author · 33

THE DISASTER

It happened early in the evening on an otherwise quiet and gentle day. Suddenly the air was filled with earth-shattering squawks and screams. Vincent van Gander determined that the awful sounds were coming from the hen house. "There's a fox in the hen house for sure," he thought. And then he raised the alarm, honking loudly. He sent a messenger to get watchdog Shasta, and then he ran for the hen house, honking for all he was worth all the way.

The other geese came quickly, converging on the location of the alarm. The geese were ready to run into the hen house, knowing that their numbers would frighten off a fox, when Shasta came racing up. He listened to the ruckus in the hen house for an instant, then ran in. All the animals by now knew that something big was happening and gathered around the hen house, waiting. A series of barks and growls followed, and almost before the fight started, the fox dashed out of the hen house and made for the woods, with Shasta on his tail.

Vincent went into the hen house, and it was more than an hour before he appeared again. Shasta was back from the (unsuccessful) chase and waiting for the news. "It's a disaster in there," Vincent began. "Two of the hens were killed, and the rest are in shock. I think it will be weeks before they begin laying eggs at any reasonable rate. This news really isn't going to go over well."

"You're right," Shasta replied. "Farmer Brown is going to learn what happened. He will not be pleased at all!

"I hate to cast blame, but Farmer Brown will," predicted Shasta. "You were in charge of the hen house, Vincent. Didn't you have a security system in place? This is just terrible. And this couldn't have come at a worse time—we are in critical times right now. We have been trying to increase productivity to make ends meet. We can't afford a hit like this. Unfortunately, this happened on your watch, so Farmer Brown will hold you responsible. For your sake, this had better not happen again!"

VINCENT'S AMAZING ALGORITHM

Vincent was very upset. Running the hen house had always been a rather nice assignment. See that the chickens were fed, see that the eggs were gathered, and see that the place got cleaned out occasionally. Once he had assigned these chores to his team of geese, not too much was demanded of him. The hen house ran profitably, and Farmer Brown admired him. But all this was now in jeopardy. He must take active steps to prevent this disaster from occurring again. And more, to regain his lost status, his plan to protect the hen house must now not only work, but be dazzling in concept.

A DAZZLING SOLUTION

"I'll post my geese as sentries," he thought. "My geese are strong and aggressive and can scare a fox away with no problem. But who…?"

"There are six geese on my staff, not counting me," he pondered. "I can't do sentry duty because I have to run things here. Four of the six don't have critical assignments right now; I can use them right away. The other two are working on the Flooded Pigsty project, which has higher priority and I hear isn't going very well. OK! We'll make do with the four. And I feel a plan forming…."

Vincent gathered the four geese and gave them their new assignments, stressing the critical importance of this project working perfectly right from the start. "There's no room for mistakes," said Vincent to the four. "I have thought this through—there is no reason for the scheme not to work from the start and forever. This scheme is bulletproof. This scheme is foolproof.

"Here's the plan. We use step stools to create sentry stations at points every 90 degrees in a large circle around the perimeter of the barnyard. Each of you geese stand on a goose step and keep an alert watch for the fox. If you see him, sound the alarm and head for the hen house. If you hear an alarm from one of the others, join in the alarm and head for the hen house."

VINCENT'S AMAZING ALGORITHM

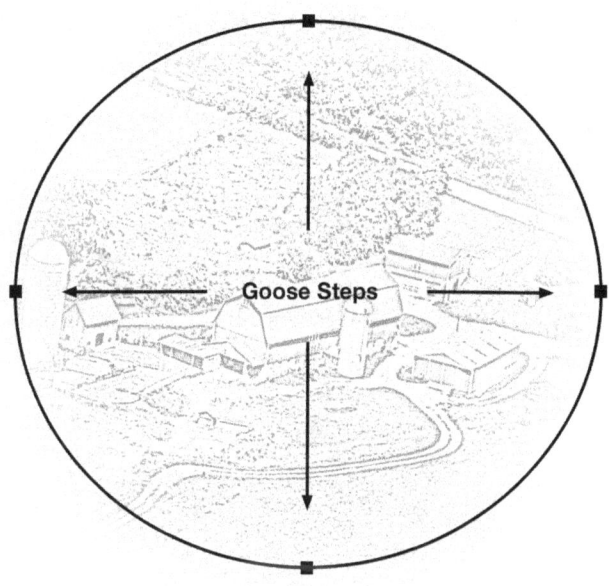

Vincent's Algorithm

Geese:
If you see the fox, sound the alarm and head for the hen house.

If you hear an alarm from one of the others, join in the alarm and head for the hen house.

The plan worked perfectly for a while, and everyone thought that Vincent was a genius. The chickens were beginning to calm down from the hen house incident and things looked fine, until…

UNFORESEEN PROBLEMS SHOW UP

Suddenly, screams and squawks arose from the hen house again. The fox had returned and claimed two more victims. Vincent investigated and found that Sara, one of the sentry geese, had fallen asleep. The fox must have waited and watched for this to occur, then taken advantage of the opportunity.

Vincent reprimanded Sara harshly. She hung her head in shame, knowing that she had been the cause of the death and destruction. She took the reprimand quietly, with a very heavy heart. She walked slowly away, as though her mind were in a fog. She couldn't bear to face the others.

Watchdog Shasta had been watching all this going on. He didn't normally interfere with Vincent's management of the geese, but seeing Sara bear her burden of guilt and shame was too much.

"Vincent, what happened wasn't Sara's fault," Shasta scolded. "Posting a single sentry on a very long watch is bound to fail sooner or later. Geese are flocking creatures, and their energy sinks low if they are alone for long periods of time. Besides, all animals need to take breaks. They should work in pairs."

"Shasta, I think you're right—pairs would work better," Vincent replied. "They can spell each other for breaks, at the very least. But there's a problem: if I station them in pairs, they won't be able to see the whole perimeter of the farm."

"Well, we could use the two geese over on the Flooded Pigsty project," Shasta offered. "This second incident has given your project visibility all the way up to Farmer Brown. He's given this sentry project top priority. I'll arrange for immediate replacements, and you work on a new plan. But be warned—Farmer Brown is pretty upset about this. There's no more room for mistakes."

VINCENT TRIES TO FIND A NEW APPROACH

Vincent studied the sentry problem with renewed vigor. Three pairs of goose steps at 120-degree spacing could be established with six geese working in pairs. There still was the visibility problem, however. The whole perimeter was barely visible using four sentry posts—three just wouldn't do it. The fox was sure to find a blind spot and would be in the hen house in a flash.

He went looking for Shasta and found him sharing a drink from the duck pond with Leed Lemming. Vincent approached them. "The sentry project will fail. We just don't have enough geese," he complained. "We're up against the laws of geometry here. Given that the geese must work in pairs, there simply are not enough geese."

Leed jumped in. "Let us do it!" he exclaimed. "There are plenty of us, and more all the time! We could do this with no problem!"

"Not so fast," said Shasta. "I'm not sure this would work. Your guys are enthusiastic workers, Leed, but they are small and defenseless, and don't make sounds. How could they scare off the fox or even raise an alarm?" Shasta turned to Vincent. "All I've ever seen the lemmings do is follow Leed in a line. They go wherever Leed goes."

"We have too few geese but plenty of lemmings," said Vincent. "There must be a way to use these lemmings to accomplish the job."

Shasta agreed. "I'm going to send for one of the independent thinkers and see if she can fix the algorithm."

TABBY HELPS OUT

The farm was lucky to have three independent feline thinkers—Fluffy, Tuffy, and Tabby. Fluffy and Tuffy were both working more than full time on the Flooded Pigsty project. Tabby was also working hard to keep up the other work of all three but agreed to consult on the sentry project.

She considered the problem and the constraints, then suggested that the geese be placed in pairs at 120-degree points in the circle and that the lemmings be placed every 10 degrees between these points to form a ring. She did some fast calculations and suggested that eleven small markers (lemming bars) be placed between each of the goose steps.

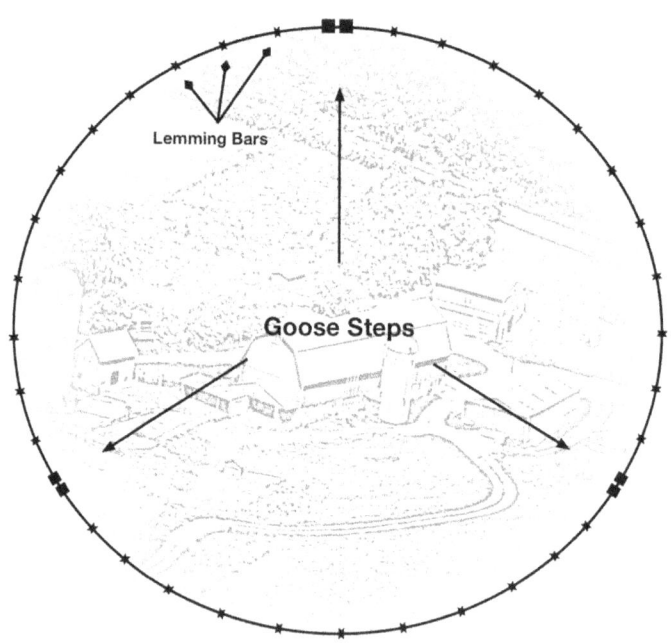

And then she laid out the rules for executing the plan.

Tabby's Algorithm

Lemmings:
If you see the fox, run to the nearest goose.

Geese:
If a lemming comes, sound the alarm and fly to the hen house.

If you hear the alarm, join in the alarm and fly to the hen house.

"Wow!" shouted Vincent. "What a concept!"

"You know," Shasta said, "those cats are remarkable—most of the time it does seem like they just lie around. But they're great to have around if you need an algorithm. Who else could have thought of such an ingenious idea? This sounds like it will work."

Vincent went to work implementing Tabby's algorithm. He placed three pairs of goose steps and 33 lemming bars in a circle around the farm and shouted, "Take your stations!"

The geese ran to their goose steps right away, but the lemmings just milled around.

"Lemmings! Take your stations!" Vincent commanded again.

But the lemmings continued in what seemed to be a random walk.

Vincent was very frustrated. He ordered two of the geese to bring Tabby over and then started placing a lemming on each lemming bar, one by one.

MORE ABOUT LEMMINGS

Shasta went off with Leed to discuss the problem. After a couple of hours, they came back and found Vincent and Tabby in a heated discussion.

Shasta interrupted: "I've been talking with Leed, and I understand a lot more about lemmings—I mean **a lot more**. A lot of stuff is beginning to make sense. It seems that a lemming's brain only has three compartments.

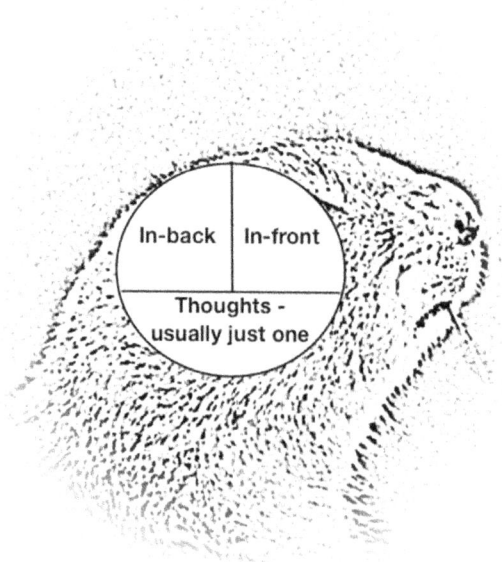

Lemming brain compartments

He can recognize the lemming in front of him (he's called in-front) and the lemming that follows him (called in-back), and the third compartment is used for thoughts. Now, the overwhelming majority of lemmings can only have one thought at a time. If another thought comes, it replaces the first. A few lemmings can have two or even three thoughts at once—Leed, for example—he's a genius in the lemming world. What we saw over there wasn't a random walk in the sense that we know it. Each lemming was following his in-front. But Leed wasn't there, and the first lemming was doing a random walk."

Tabby was astonished. "I'm beginning to understand why the lemmings haven't performed all that well on other projects. In fact, it's hard to see how they could do anything at all. How in the world can they survive? Does each really only recognize his in-front and his in-back? That would imply that any one lemming only recognizes two other lemmings in the whole pack."

"In their natural world, they do just fine," Shasta explained. "In fact, this tends to keep them out of trouble. Leed usually heads up the chain, and he makes all the plans. And he puts one of the smartest lemmings at the tail. Each individual really only sees two other lemmings, since they are in a line, so this all makes sense. This obviously works, since there are so many lemmings. More all the time, in fact."

"What happens when a lemming dies and the chain is broken? What happens when new lemmings are born? This is fascinating."

"No problem. If a lemming dies, everyone sits down and Leed introduces the dead lemming's in-back to his in-front. Each replaces the information in the appropriate brain compartment, and everything goes on as before. New lemmings are added to the end of the chain, just before the tail lemming, with Leed introducing them in turn."

"Well, I could listen to this for hours," Tabby said, "but let's get practical. Vincent needs to have this information. His plan will never succeed unless we allow for these limitations. The algorithm we have could never have worked—give me a few minutes to think about this." She jumped on the fence and curled up in a ball.

TABBY SOLVES THE GEOMETRY PROBLEM

She looked for all the world to be napping, but soon Tabby jumped up and said, "I've got it! We can live within these limitations, but it's going to be pretty complicated. I see now that the old algorithm could never have worked. We'll have to scrap the whole thing. We will first conceptually transform the line of lemmings into a ring!

"And then we will have to come up with a change to the algorithm."

Tabby told the lemmings to form their natural line. Then she had Leed walk round the circle clockwise and leave each lemming at a lemming bar until there was a lemming on each one.

"Now, each of you is standing on a lemming bar and can see your in-front and your in-back."

Leed looked forward and saw the tail of the chain! His head was spinning with the thought that the tail of the chain was now his in-front. As smart as he was, he found the ring concept almost beyond understanding.

Tabby's Revised Algorithm

Lemmings:
If you see the fox, go to your in-front.

If your in-back comes, go to your in-front.

Geese:
If a lemming runs by, then sound the alarm and fly to the hen house.

If you hear the alarm, join in the alarm and fly to the hen house.

"This is getting pretty complicated," Shasta said. "It's been my experience that unexpected and bad things happen when things get too complex."

But Vincent was excited. The lemmings were finally in place, he had Tabby's new algorithm, and he could implement his new security system. It was hard to figure out how to test the new system, though, without a fox.

But this seemed really foolproof. "We'll go with this," he said.

But the fox was back in the hen house almost immediately. The fox had simply killed a lemming and walked right through the sentry border.

"What in the world happened?" Shasta wondered. "How could this possibly have failed?"

"Let's try and think this through," said Vincent. "There is obviously something wrong with the algorithm. Let's just try and take each step. Now, when the fox killed the lemming, surely his in-front or in-back would have noticed. He obviously would have seen the fox. And his logic tells him to go to his in-front when he sees the fox. I don't know—this should have worked."

VINCENT'S AMAZING ALGORITHM

"Uh oh, wait a minute," said a chastened Tabby. "If the dead lemming's in-front saw the fox, it might work because he should go to his in-front. But if only his in-back saw the fox, he couldn't do anything because then his in-front would be dead and the chain would be broken. But it's even worse than that. I just realized that none of the lemmings could even recognize the fox at all. They can only recognize other lemmings, and only two at that. Egad. Back to the drawing board. Sorry about that."

"Great—an algorithm full of holes. It couldn't possibly have worked. How is Farmer Brown going to react to this?" groaned Vincent.

TABBY GETS THINGS MOVING

Now Tabby was lost in thought, deeply absorbed with the algorithm. It must cover every case. And the limitations were staggering. Even if a lemming saw a fox, there was no way to get the information to any of the geese, since no recognition ever took place.

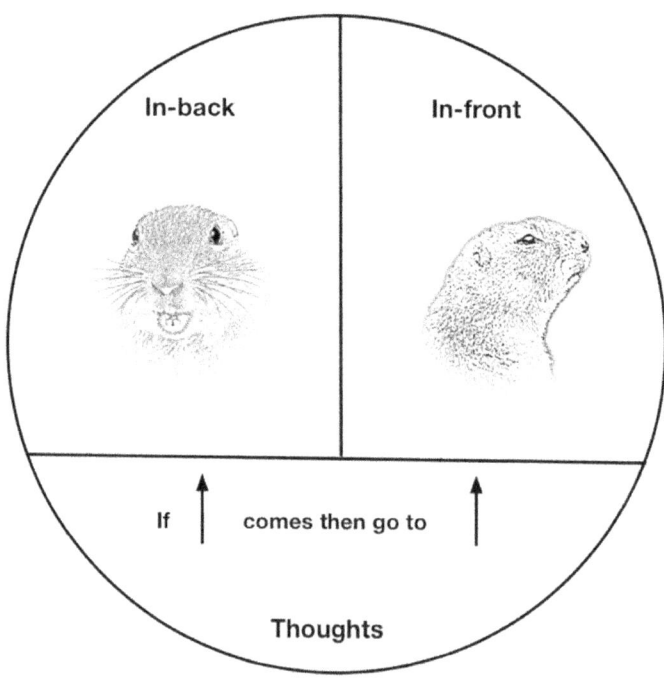

Lemming brain compartments again

Working with the limitations

VINCENT'S AMAZING ALGORITHM

So how could the geese find out if a lemming saw a fox?

Would it be safe to assume that if the fox was that close that he would kill the lemming? That was what had happened so far. All right! Now we have a dead lemming, but how could the geese discover that this had happened?

What if the ring were set in motion? The lemmings could run from one lemming bar to the next around the ring. Leed could initiate the action by running to his in-front (formerly the tail of the line).

Here's the way it could work (given the limitations of the lemmings' brains): when a lemming's in-back arrives, he would run to his in-front. If a lemming was killed, his in-front would not get started. That would be the only information that could possibly be passed on in this event.

But how could the stopping of the motion be determined?

Hmmm...What about using a countdown, starting at a countdown maximum value and going to zero?

Each goose would simply start counting down from a countdown max value and reset to the max value whenever a lemming ran by. If the countdown ever went to zero, it would mean that the ring motion had stopped, that a lemming had been killed, and that the fox was on his way to the hen house.

Tabby asked Vincent to determine the countdown max value.

Tabby's Updated Revised Algorithm

Lemmings:
When your in-back comes, go to your in-front.

Geese:
Start counting down from 110.

If a lemming comes before you reach zero then start counting all over at 110; else, if you reach zero then sound the alarm and fly to the hen house.

If you hear the alarm, join in the alarm and fly to the hen house.

And so they implemented the updated algorithm. Things worked perfectly all morning, but the alarm sounded about noon. The geese flew to the hen house, and all the animals rushed over.

But there was no fox—not in the hen house, nor anywhere around the sentry ring. So the sentry animals went back to work. And then another false alarm happened several days later.

And then another several days after that. But there was never a fox in sight. Curious…

"What could be causing the false alarms?" thought Tabby. "Let's see. The alarm goes off when the countdown goes to zero. The countdown max accounts for the sum of counts it takes for a lemming to run from one goose step to another. Hmmm…"

"Vincent! How did you calculate the countdown max?"

"Well, I had a lemming run between two lemming bars, counted all the while and got to 10, then multiplied by 11 to get 110," answered Vincent, originally proud of this contribution to the algorithm, but now feeling his stomach beginning to sink. "Do you think there's a problem with my math?"

"Actually, the math sounds fine. What could it be? Hmmmm…" pondered Tabby. "Let's measure again just to make sure."

TABBY SOLVES THE TIMING PROBLEM

They reconstructed Vincent's timing experiment. Vincent counted while the lemming ran from his bar to his in-front, and got 30. "I know I counted at the same rate. Dumb lemming. Probably not a good sample point. Let's try another." Which they did, but still got 30.

Shasta watched this whole experiment. "Don't you see what's going on? These guys are exhausted. They run around in circles all day long. You performed your timing analysis on a fresh lemming. They won't be able to keep up that pace all day long. Luckily the hen house is locked all night, or things would be even worse! Let's ask Tabby to analyze this problem." Which Tabby did that very day.

Tabby came back with an answer. "This timing problem has many aspects," said Tabby. "If the countdown max is too short, we get false alarms—the geese fly to the hen house when the fox isn't even there. If the max is too long, we won't know if the fox got to the hen house until it's too late. Since the time between each lemming bar is 30 counts and there are 11 lemming bars between goose steps, let's make the countdown max 11 times 30 or 330.

"I think we probably have the kinks all worked out now," Tabby said hopefully.

And so Vincent's latest algorithm was implemented with the new countdown max. All the animals were tense, waiting to see what would go wrong next. But, as time went by, there was never even one instance where the fox got to the hen house. The annoying constant false alarm problem had also gotten much, much better.

There was a false alarm once a week or so, but the fox was never seen.

QUITTERS!

"Probably a tired lemming who quit," Vincent would say. "We know about that problem. Quitters! Lemmings can be lazy guys who don't give their all!"

Shasta and Tabby were walking in the pasture and talking about the sentry problem. "This scheme seems to be working pretty well," said Shasta. "I guess the only thing that really bothers me about this method is that the lemmings work to the point of exhaustion as the nominal plan. And we seem to have a lemming just give up and quit once a week or so. It just doesn't feel right."

"Yes, I know. It bothers me too," Tabby answered. "We should work something out. We do have a lot of lemmings, many more than we can fit on the bars. The rest just sit by and watch. They seem not to mind too much."

"When a lemming goes missing, Leed just takes one of the standby lemmings, puts him into the empty slot, and introduces him to his new in-front and in-back," Shasta mused. "They smile and carry on. Remember that they can only absorb one thought at a time, so they don't think much about their missing comrade. *But we never seem to see the one who quit.*"

Shasta thought on this for a while. "Why do we never see him? My guess is that he doesn't want to be known as the guy who let the ring down. I'm betting that he falls in with the waiting lemmings, none of which know him. And once he's replaced, even his in-front and in-back won't know him, since the information in their brain compartments will have been replaced. Makes sense to me."

"This whole dynamic is pretty poor, though," Tabby replied. "With all these spare lemmings, we should work to get a replacement scheme that's a little more elegant. Perhaps we could work them in shifts. Let me think some more on this."

"Well, in any case, we learned a lot about the lemmings," Shasta added. "But now I see why they always seemed to get into so much trouble on their previous assignments. I just didn't know. It's mostly my fault, really. You have to be very careful what you ask them to do."

AND SO THE STORY ENDS

The fox never again invaded the hen house, and the false alarm problem had been reduced to once a week or so. *They never were able to figure out a fix to the algorithm for this false alarm.*

Tabby found herself in a strange situation. Farmer Brown had somehow gotten the impression that Vincent had solved the problem alone. On the one hand, Tabby felt a little burned that her work was not recognized. On the other hand, the sentry problem had been challenging and kind of fun to solve.

"I think I made a mistake in that I started with Vincent's algorithm and kept fixing the errors," she told Shasta. "I should have started from scratch when they first asked me to help. I think that maybe just stationing two geese at the hen house might have done the trick.

"But this actually seems to be working pretty well, now that we've found all the errors. And the lemmings seem so happy...."

And for the others, it was a win-win-win-win-win solution:

The geese had rather nice assignments, where most of the time they chatted with their partners but got occasional episodes of swift flying and loud honking, all of which geese just love to do.

The lemmings got an assignment that was perfect for them, since they loved nothing better than running in a circle, one behind the other, all day long—and they gained the respect of the barnyard.

The chickens got used to the new serenity of the hen house and even began to believe they were safe forever. They laid eggs at a record-breaking rate.

Vincent got an award from Farmer Brown. He was very, very, very proud.

The scheme worked out pretty well for the fox too. It turned out that he found the lemmings quite tasty.

Once a week or so…

ABOUT THE AUTHOR

Michele Downs graduated with a BA and MS in mathematics from San Jose State University in 1978 and 1980, respectively. She has nearly thirty years of experience in software engineering, program management, and functional management. She has developed and taught corporate training courses in software development and engineering methodology. She has served as a software engineering methodology consultant for a wide variety of software programs.

She has four grown children and six grandchildren and currently lives in the Santa Cruz Mountains in California.

www.ingramcontent.com/pod-product-compliance
Lightning Source LLC
Chambersburg PA
CBHW072045190526
45165CB00018B/1838